....in
spite
of
my
Generation

———————

Matt Ross

….in spite of my Generation
Copyright © 2014 by Matthew Ross

ISBN (978-0-9921002-1-6)

Printed by Dead Sparrow Press

Dead Sparrow Press

**Dedicated
to my generation
in spite
of
my
generation**

Table of Contents

Listen to all

Follow one

Introduction

People say my poetry is vile, sick, perverted, hypocritical, judgmental, badly written, unstructured, no form, not poetry, deep, honest, hilarious, descriptive, doesn't rhyme and on and on. They may be right but in my world it doesn't matter what people think. What matters is honesty. Too many people think a poem starts with roses are red and violets are blue or have to rhyme. I think of a place to puke when I see roses and rhyming poetry, in my opinion, lacks authenticity. I write about what's happening in my life, the feelings in my gut, the thoughts in my head, the things I find funny like shitting at work or a terrible experience in public or ass grabbing or drinking or the inconsistencies in the media or society or the government or what life is or is not supposed to be. I write about love and hard ons, anger, fear, loneliness and anxiety. I wonder about god, science, religion, evolution and truth.

It seems there's truth and lies in most things.

One absolute truth I acknowledge is death.

Everything else is just what happened before it.

Matt Ross

The Spite of My Generation

Generation
Y
Bother?

....in spite of my Generation

I want to thank you for nothing
The future is a lie
I'm lost in a city full of people
in a world full of maps
in a universe made of stars
in the galaxy of the mind
in the milky way of existence
on the cusp of heaven
in the stream of eternity
thinking about the weight of emptiness
laughing at myself in the mirror
I rise from half-sleep into conscious reality
Only to hear the echo's of car horns and unfulfilled dreams
Nine-to-five 'til you die sounds like a bad country song to me
Here's the path you thought you'd take
Go to University
thinking when you finish
you'll find a high paying
interesting job
that you like
Get married to a person who'll stay young and beautiful forever
Raise a family of decent children
who'll have a better life then you did
Not realizing
your education means very little
It's who you know that gets you the job
The life mate isn't as pretty as you thought
They get old and fat just like yourself
You can only afford one child you pay someone else to raise
Your kid ain't as great as you thought they'd be but you like
them anyways cuz they'll keep you company in your later years
The job doesn't pay enough
The work not nearly as stimulating
The days of your future bleakly similar
Your kids will have kids and the cycle will repeat to infinity
or the end of time which ever comes first
In spite of my generation I yawn at this reality
This robotic oblivion of the soul
I yawn at the boringness of perfection
A family photo at Walmart pretty much sums it up
With their Sunday school bests and smiles for the camera
Perfectly lame

Not learning from the mistakes of the parents
Divorced unhappy families of resentment
Abandoned by youth
Abducted by middle then old age
Wondering what happened to all the years
Staring at your 40 year old University educated child who's still
living at home because they have no where else to go
Looking at your mortgage statement at 65 years old depressed
by the 20 years remaining on the amortization
At least you can still masturbate and drink alone
Wake up to go to a job you hate to make money for a family
you love while the Haves' feast on your labour
with their private jets
Mansions
Cottages
Savings
Golf Trips
Celebrity friends
Superbowls
Well dressed children
In tact childhood dreams
Trophy wives
and bright futures
While you punch in
and grind it out 'til your first 15 minute break
Get a smoke or coffee
Talk to colleagues who you would normally never talk to but do
due to circumstance
Grind 'til lunch
Take your last break
Grind Monday
Grind Tuesday
Grind Wednesday
Drink with friends after work
Check out the hot waitress's
Hit on them or at least flirt
Grind the commute
Grind out Friday
Enjoy the weekend
Week after week until your first of 3 weeks of vacation a year
Grind 'til a long weekend
Grind day in and day out 'til all remaining is death
Soon your once invincible parents begin to fade before your
eyes

Your Dad the fisherman
The Hunter
The Question Answerer
The one person you looked up to the most
Who taught much of what you know
or your mother
are gone
You imagine a world without them which makes you sad
What would you do without them?
They say the moment you lose a parent is the moment you
realize your own mortality
Yes
even you will die
So will your kids and their kids and their kids until there are no
more kids
Don't be upset with death
It's the one thing that brings life meaning
Everything ends
This makes every breath
every conversation
every hug or kiss
every shit
every joke
every moment
Magnificent
The fact you could be dead tomorrow is motivation to live today
Go for it
Whatever it is
Don't wait
Cuz' time
is
the greatest killer of all

Nothin'

What's wrong with doin nothing?
Sittin on the couch
Relaxin
Playin guitar
Listening to Laurel Canyon folklore
and conspiracies
So many people dead
Intelligent crimes I'm sure
Smokin
Eatin pizza
and chicken
Cleaning out the drain of the tub
Pullin out a hairy grey sludge of doughy filth
Realizing why the drain didn't work so well
Writin' and singin songs like "Upside down"
and
"The Future is your Past"
Imagining packed shows
Screamin audiences
Sweat
Beer
Chicks
Rock and Roll
Kissing Blonde Haired Blue Eyed Gurls
Ebony Princesses
and German Broomhilda's
Life dreamin reality in a world created by me
The Pied Piper
Rages' glory
Decision Maker
Ohhhhh,
Sweet destiny
how I loathe the hero of your play

1981

GSP
Michael Pitt
Eli Manning
Natalie Portman
Belladonna
Clay Guida
Britney Spears
Matt Ross
Justin Timberlake
Jessica Alba
Sienna Miller
Elijah Wood
Amy Lee
Serena Williams
Beyonce Knowles
Adriana Lima
Dany Heatley
Roger Federer
Somehow Matt Ross will never fit in on this list
Is he
the Writer
the Liver
the Voice
the Reason
of his generation?
If so is he also a reflection?
A representation
A combatant
A participant in the destruction
or deconstruction
of a way of thinking,
possibly your way of thinking?
Naw

Manager of the Year

When I took the job in I never thought my life would end up like this, broke, bored and ridden like a whore on a hard on. Dreams like youth disappear with each day. I wish I had nightmares about the future so I wouldn't be disappointed when they didn't come true. Not that it really matters because if a dream did come true it'd probably end as nightmare anyways.

I sit at my desk and stare at the screen. It's 2:51pm. I hear voices of employees talking to clients about mortgages or to those in the know, death pledges. One's selling it and the others begging for it. Both lose. Pay 'til you die sounds like a shitty philosophy to me but who am I to judge! I'm the degenerate managing this operation. I don't know how many people I've enslaved with debt but it doesn't matter, a man's gotta eat.

There are some perks. I work with some real characters. They're all kinda in the same boat as me, slowly filling with water, stranded in the middle of an ocean drifting aimlessly waiting for death or termination which ever comes first. The problem is most of them have families to feed, wives to clothe, vacations to pay for, credit cards, phone bills, car loans and everything else in between. Nothing in this life is free except birth and death and even then you have to pay the price of pain. Life is shit then you die. That's just how it is. You can never really start your life until you figure this fact out.

I should probably introduce you to myself. My name is Mitch Ruger, I'm a bank manager, musician, writer, a success and failure all at the same time. I used to think money and title made the man but in reality those men are just inglorious slaves. Now that I realize this, I can enjoy the finer things; booze, pussy, cigarettes and not giving a fuck about much. Sure I need money so I have to put minimal effort in at work just like Bukowski.

Work the addiction of the masses, why have you forsaken me? What have I done to deserve this cruel punishment? Sales targets, stats, employees and meetings of pure horror. If this is life then I don't wanna know what Hell is gonna be like. The Devil might be an improvement from upper management or the Overseer's as I like to call them, with their tag lines and motto's like "Trust, Synergy and Responsibility", while they hire a "Quality Support Team" to watch and listen to our every move. Not unlike Orwell's 1984.

Disturbing as this may sound, this is the grim work environment I am a part of. A mid level manager with little sway who gets shit on from above and pissed on from below. Kind of like a stacked human port-a-potty that I'm stuck in the middle of. The Overseer's are concerned with one thing, profit. Doesn't matter how they get it just as long as they do. The catch is we have to do it within their guidelines and policies which are made up as they go along and enforced by the "Quality Support Team" or The Enforcers as they're known on the floor. With their bald headed leader Tom Chip who looks like Uncle Fester except dressed in a sweater vest. A figure that stands behind the powerful overseer's and shrivels up when confronted by anyone outside the virtual world. He's a majestic beast on email and a leftover turd in the bowl in real life. All you need to do is flush and he's gone.

What's scarier then the A-Bomb?

What's scarier then the A-Bomb?
        The Fall of the American Dollar!
No more something for nothing
An entire system collapsing in a day
People, death
and burning
will be the new entertainment
Your shitty little desk job obsolete
No more super markets full of food
No more welfare checks
No more right
     to live like a
               materialistic vulture
                         feeding on the bones
                              of a once fat society
     Your economy full of ulcers
               rips at you like a whip through a slaves back
Water runs brown
Animals retreat deep into forests and jungles
Breed and grow strong
Your once mighty streets get covered in moss and grass
Powerful monuments grow into strange gardens
While the animals bide their time
You think about all the other once great civilizations
and realize everything dies
Ideas
Culture
Civilizations
Stars
Galaxies
Planets
Gods
Earths
Flowers
and
You

Freedom of the Joker

You are alone
You are a freak
You are angry
You are a mistake
You are magnetic
You are water
You are divine
You are the center of the universe
Every where you go the sun shines on you
The moon glows for you
The birds sing
and the bee's buzz
and the wind blows
and the drama and happiness
and rejection
and death
and everything
u n f o l d s
f o r
y
o
u

Google Search

Big black booty
Is Tom Cruise gay?
Does Paris Hilton have herpes?
Celebrities with herpes
How to enlarge your penis?
Is Obama a Muslim?
Miley Cyrus twerking
Actual twerking
Leafs score
Raptors score
How to score?
Matthew Ross
What kind of loser googles his own name?
Nietzsche
Bukowski
What's the meaning of life?
Does God exist?
    It seems Google knows everything
        Is some sort of information Devil
    Google will one day be renamed Googod
    and worshipped
    Sacrifices will be made
    New civilizations born
    and
    Googod will rule them with an electronic fist
All Hail Googod
All Hail Googod
All Hail Googod

Born in a World of Hate

Born in a World of Hate
while Angels eat the faces of Angels
while Holy men do unholy things
while Presidents feed the poor
to
the rich
    While Devils learn from men
    No longer the seducer but the seduced
    While children are left to fend for themselves
    only to succumb to the whims of nature
    While your fat belly rumbles for more
                     nations die from less
    While progress becomes a march to oblivion
    While school gurls sell their bodies for lip stick and tampons
    While it's cheaper to kill then it is to save
    While prisons and hospitals become profitable corporations
    While governments are the greatest killer of all
    Three hundred million and counting
    Kind of like McDonalds
    One day a billion will be served
    While you'd rather have safe slavery
                 over
                  obnoxious
                    freedom
              The church bells ring
              The sun rises
              The ocean does its thing
                and
              God wonders
              what went
              wrong?

What comes before?

Hate usually comes before murder
Love before hate
At times interchangeable
Misguided love
  is as dangerous
    as misguided hate
 Think about
   how much
     Americans
       love America
        and hate Muslims
   Where love blooms
      hate blossoms
Flowers save and flowers kill
     Same with humans
No matter how beautiful
   or sweet something is
     doesn't mean it can't hurt you
   Ugliness the cure
   Hatred the savior
   Love the impaler
While the whole world waits for the future
they forget the past and ignore the present
  And we wonder why everything's
   gone to shit

The Asylum of Earth

Born in the asylum of earth
A patient in the land of time
Slowly waking up to how it all works
Rich people
scum bags
politicians
lying
murdering thieves at the top
And the rest of us
at the bottom
Also scumbags, liars and thieves
Rippin and pullin at eachother for the scraps
Begging to be house slaves
plantation owners
bank managers
the fucking mayor
Each day chasin money
houses
cars
other people's dreams.
For what?
Status
Comfort
Narcissism
Ego fulfillment
We'll destroy the whole planet for a few bucks
While the devil sleeps
Man takes his place on the perch
Overlooking the whole damned operation
meticulously
gladly
orgasmically
and
smiling
always
smiling

The Scratched Record of Life (The Same or Similar)

You ever get the feeling your life has become a loop?
Doing similar things in familiar places
You start your job at the same time
Work similar hours
with similar colleagues
eating the same thing
hangin at the same bar
with the same waitress's (most of which you won't sleep with)
Tellin stories about the last time you were at the same place
You go on the same vacation
                            every year to where you're from
With people you no longer have much in common with
They think you need to grow up
              but deep down know
                  it's themselves
                      who've given up
Now they herd together
Live the same lives
Watch the same football team
Go to the same birthday parties
Watch the same TV show every Sunday
                  or Football every Monday night
The Elite understand
                  entertainment is the greatest
                      form of
                          enslavement
        So many people think
              if they move outta
                    their parents
                        house into a
                            condo downtown
                                things'll change
You expect new order and all you get is old chaos
You crave change
To break the loop you need to do different things in that loop
Rather then watching your favorite TV show
                      maybe write a journal
              or practice guitar or go for a walk
                      or do something different
        You need to diversify
                but in the end your world
                      may feel like one giant loop anyways

Unless you change your mindset
to
   you're on a journey
                   and everything you do is destiny
A thought in your head
               becoming flesh
                     blood
               and smelly reality
                   is a real
                   possibility
         Actualization of your inner most desires can happen
         Your life is a magnificent sojourn into the unknown
            If you look at your life like this
               You may find yourself
                  in the very place
                  you thought most
                     impossible
                        of
                        all

Footnote Nope

You won't even be a footnote in anyone's history book
Your life doesn't deserve to be remembered
Time will forget you
All that will be left of you is dust
and
even the dust
won't be
swept away

The Age of Decadence

They say Empires last 250 years

10 generations

Comprised of 6 ages

The Age of Exploration
The Age of Invasion
The Age of Trade
The Age of Prosperity
The Age of Intellect
The Age of Decadence

We are in the Age of Decadence now

Sex obsessed
Bemused by spectacles
Sports
Violence
Gluttony
Degeneracy
Excess
Evil
Vulgarity
Decline
The time when the drugs don't work
They are needed just to move forward
One percent of the people have 99% of the money
We have more money in circulation then the United States from
1776 to 2008 when Obama took over
We have access to anything we want at the touch of a button
Western people are dying from obesity while nations starve
Extreme sports killing people every day
War is commonplace
America started in 1776
We are in year 238 of this empire
Where is the world gonna be in 2026?

Built to last

Manufacturing
products
that were
built to last
used to be a motto
of early Capitalism
Until profitability dominated the idea
Why are
we building
one very
good car
that could last
20 years
when we could build
one acceptable car
make minor changes
year over year
call it the new model
and sell
the same
shitty car
with a 5 year shelf life
year after year
every year
and make
record profits
forever
Until not even
the earths resources
can keep up
until the earth itself
is disposed of

Apocalypse of the Mind

What if most things you believe true, aren't?
History a lie
Christopher Columbus
The villain not the hero
The conqueror not the explorer
News isn't here to inform but misinform
Government's purpose is mind control
Education teaches you to follow
What if I told you the truth is real
          but you don't get to choose what is or is not true
The truth simply IS.
You will die
This cannot be denied and is the truth
Show me a man who's lived forever
and I'll show you a liar and a fool
Peace and liberty are the causes of most wars
Presidents, Dictators, Prime Ministers
All leaders of countries are Patsy's
Fall guys for the real people who call the shots
If something goes wrong blame them
Leaders change but the machine behind them does not
Think of them as hood ornaments on a car
If something happens to the hood ornament
the car still runs
Money is debt not wealth
It costs a thousand dollars to print a billion
Backed by what?
What collateral could allow this?
You
Your body
Your mind
Your labour
Your person
Your slavery by consent
or ignorance
either way
you're not free

Generation Coward

Don't you see what they're doing?
With all these anti-bullying commercials and laws!
Pretending to be helping the kids
All they're doing is turning them into cowards
Teaching people to look to authority figures to give them justice
Ratting and finger pointing being hailed as the right thing to do
They're raising a generation of cowards
Order waiters
Imagine how easy it would be to control a bunch of people who
don't know how to defend themselves?
Like a razor through soft flesh
When you're in trouble you're trained to call 911
                   rather then to pick up a baseball bat
                      and crush the intruders skull
Taught not sticking up for yourself is strength
                   or letting a friend get shit kicked
               and run for help
               rather then help
Watching Police Officers beat up whoever they want
Used by the government to suppress and control us like pests
An entire generation of rats in need of exterminating
Have you ever thought the President's
                   and Prime Minister's are Pied Pipers
                     and you're the children being
                         led to the slaughter?
          I didn't think so
          You might wanna start

Stumblin'
drunk
nights
and
hangover
fueled
days

The Horror and the Alcohol

Get off work Thursday
5pm
Go to Austin's Steakhouse
Order beer
Drink two an hour 'til 10pm
Get hammered
Tell women I like them
Tell friends to shut up
Make obscene comments like
"He sings best with a mouth full of cocks"
or
"Her vagina just threw up"
Find myself transforming
into a hard drinking
grizzled Bukowskiesque
dirty old man-clown at the party
Pay bill
Tip well
Stumble out of the bar in silent rage
Get on street car
Puke
Read book of Kerouac letters
Relate to his belligerence and brilliance
Arrive home
Rent documentary about Salinger
Drink water
Jerk off
Text my ebony princess
Pass out
Wake up
Hungover
Hard
and
thursty
for
more

Wow

What is this?
This madness
This headache
This pit in my stomach
This hangover eating away at me
Did I really need to go that hard?
Work is gonna suck more than normal today
And I got to go to another party tonight
I feel like puking
The only thing worse then a bad hangover
is no hangover at all
Blahhhhh......

I don't care

I don't care if ur Jewish
I don't care if ur Muslim
or Christian
or Hindu
or short
or tall
or beautiful
or ugly
or straight
or gay
or male
or female
or young
or old
Doesn't matter
You be you
I'll be me
Let's have a beer
If you don't want to that's fine
I'll drink alone

Ass Grabbin'

Rape is wrong
Violence as well
Even tittie touchin without permission ain't right
But grabbin a waitress's ass at the bar
I'm cool with that
      What is an ass anyways?
      Just a hunk of flesh covering an asshole
      Kinda like a face
I mean what do you tip for?
         The service....
Come on people
     you can't tell me
 you're not disappointed
        when an ugly chick
           or a dude serves you
You'll never find a successful bar called "Ugly Chick's", will you?
Hooters ya
Tilted Kilt ya
Booty's (I wish)
There's nothin
     like gettin
   a big hunk of meat
    in one hand
    and
    a beer
     in the
      other
    There's sumpin
        about it
          I just like

Gurls?

Feel it out
Go with the gut
Have no fear
Be patient
Expect nothin
Gain everything
Timing and boldness require patience and opportunity
Victory and defeat are the same thing
To have never fought is the biggest failure of all

86t

I 86t myself from a bar recently
Austin's Steakhouse on Yonge
I'd rather eat a shitscicle then go back
Why?
Not because of the bar because I do love the bar
Not because of management or the owners because I love both
Not because of the waitresses because they're all beautiful
Not because of the outrageous prices
                    because I'll pay a premium for beauty
Not because of all the suit and tie douchebags
                                    because
                                they never
                                    bother me
        It's because I don't like being told what to do
            Anybody
                that gets
                    in my face
                        and
                    tells me
                        what to do
                            I dislike
                Authority upsets me
    I'd rather live in a brutal free world then a comfy prison
                See ya tomorrow

Cookin for a 30 Something Single Male

Open freezer
Look through frozen food
    If you're rich enough you got M&M Meat products
    Meat loaf mini's
    Breaded Louisiana Chicken Wings
    Dry Garlic pork
    Corn Dogs
    French Fries
    Sausage
    Pizza pops
Pick any combination of these things out
Put'em in the oven at 350 degrees for 25 minutes
Take'em out and eat
or
if you're exceptionally lazy
order fried chicken with fries and gravy
                  right to your door
      Turn on the Jays game
          and watch
       Joey Bats hit back to back jacks
           Bon appétit

Slow down before I speed up

I say things on my mind
whatever they may be
Sometimes good
Sometimes bad
Sometimes nice
Sometimes mean
It comes from a furnace of gentle anger
burning in my inner core
stoked by the coal spirits of the world
talking to me
hangin out with me
laughin and judging me
waitin for me to do something
Until one day they've had enough of me
Go outta their way not to see me
Duck and hide in the street from me
Rolling with old friends
Real friends
Talkin bout music and gurls and birthday parties
and days gone by
One day they'll find themselves sittin on a couch
watching TV and there I'll be
Like a lucid dream
all the times we had come flashing back
and they'll have realized far too late
those times we had
were the best times
of their lives

Where?

I used to think running around being the center of attention
Laughin
Cracking jokes
Picking up girls
Entertaining the crowd with music
Stories
Poetry
The feats of a man stumbling through time with an
ever-changing cast of characters interacting with the world
watchin it explode like an a-bomb
in the mushroom cloud wake of my life
rippling through the generations with a single expression
"Mmmm...."

was cool.

Close the blinds

Sometimes a man just don't wanna see outside
He closes the blinds
Turns off his phone
Avoids the internet
Smokes a little
Puts on a documentary
Lays on the couch
Plays guitar
Sings
Jerks
Warms up food
Takes hot bath
Relaxes
Writes
Exists
Thinks about nothin
and lets it flow
Lets it flow
Lets it flow

Socially Anti-Social

Ask anybody that knows me
and they'll tell you I'm a very social
funny
articulate
sexy
exciting
talented
degenerate
asshole
driven
prick
ego maniac
self absorbed
trustworthy
reliable
In control of the out
Basturd they've ever met
They'll say I'm socially anti-social
and they love, hate and
accept me for it

The Unflushable Turd

Not again
The Turd Burglar
Third stall on the right
There it is
Green and piled up like an innocent vagrant
Staring up at me with envy
Me staring back in disgust
I do everyone a favor and flush
(with my foot of course)
Dry heave a bit
Look forward to watchin the thing spiral into the abyss
But what's this?
A Christmas miracle
The thing doesn't move
Stubborn basturd
I go for another flush but to my amazement

It stays put

Intrigued I go back to the office

Get some colleagues to look at this absurd beast

One by one my co-workers flush to no avail

This piece of shit won't budge

You can lead a turd to water

                but you can't make him drink kinda thing
Humbled by this Unflushable Turd
I leave the
Magnificent Basturd
alone
in all it's glory
for everyone to see
Shine on little turd
Shine on

What
I want

I'll do what I want
                when I want
  If u don't like it
            I'll leave

Suicide Gurl

She was half Jamaican and Ukrainian
Short buzzed curly dyed blonde hair
Tattoos all over her body
Sugar skull with wings on her chest
She had the tightest lil body I'd ever seen
Her ass was big and round
An anomaly really
Like a soft bolt on the end of a screw
She liked her drugs
The first time I met her she was flyin on MDMA
Face flush red
Mood tempered
She sat on the couch with me
We talked for hours about different things
Her background
Brother
The meaning behind her colored scars as she called them
She asked about my music and writing
She snorted cocaine with a tampon applicator
Her drug dealer lived down the hall from me
White South African guy
A real durtbag of a person
He would yell at her
Tell her to never come back
He was mad she wouldn't fuck him or any of his "friends"
Apparently he was raped by his dealer at his place
After picking up she'd come 2 doors down to my place
Knock
I'd let her in
We'd drink beer together
She'd play Goth Electronica music
Dance a strange lonely dance
Apparently that's how people moved at the parties she went to

I would watch her sexy body jiggle

Her ass would bounce like perfect jelly

She would lay on the couch with me

Always doing more and more blow

She would kiss me

We'd make out for hours

I'd grab her ass

She'd take off her pants
All she'd wear around my place was a tank top and g-string
She told me to put on a song
I played "Black Hole Sun" by Soundgarden
and asked her to dance with me
slow like high school
She said she never danced like that before
She put her head on shoulder and we moved slowly together
She had a tear in her eye
I held her close 'til the song was over
She'd end up doin drugs all night
                              while I just hung out with her
            Eventually she'd leave
We did this on and off for months
            until her drug dealer was busted and forced to move
She'd stop by periodically afterwards
                        until she disappeared altogether
I can't even remember her name anymore
I remember she looked like a suicide gurl
A beautiful suicide gurl

Grizzled

A grizzled old man walks down Queen in Parkdale
Hunched over in a puffy winter jacket
Hands in pockets
Mean look on face
Arguing with self and losing
White hair
Beard
Snarling
Eyes moving left to right
Paranoid of himself
He talks with no one and can't understand why they don't listen
Aggravated he finds a cigarette butt on the ground
Lights it up
sits on the curb
and
enjoys one of the few pleasures he still has left in life

Killin themselves to get on the Streetcar

People never cease to amaze me
Just when I think we've bottomed out in stupidity
and selfishness
something happens to eclipse all that's come before
I'm at the Queen and Spadina stop
Everyone that's gettin off
gets off
and other people get on
The light's green so the Streetcar begins to creep forward
Cars begin passing it
Out of the blue
this pretty Indian gurl jumps in the middle of traffic
        waving her arms
A car has to swerve around her
Oblivious to her near death experience
                she demands to be let on the Streetcar
The driver stops and lets her on
"Didn't you see me?" she says
                in an ungrateful bitch of a tone
The driver ignores her
.......I think I got it bad.......
These fuckers got eat shit
        and pretend it's ice-cream everyday
At least I can tell the riders to shut up or move away from them
Imagine if your job was driving an entire generation of people
to jobs they hate
to support lives they're repulsed by
in a world they think owes them something
taking their shit day in and day out
year after year
with a big fake smile on your face
No thanks

Offensive

I met a gurl at a bar recently when I was drunk
I started talkin to her
She told me she just bought some sandals
I looked at them
Not bad
Noticed they were made in China and said
"To China, keeping their children employed so we can own shit
we don't need and look good doing it"
The gurl just kinda looked at me
Not sure if she should be insulted or offended by my comment
"Pardon me" she said in an appalled tone
"China has sweat shops full of children making stuff like those
sandals you bought. It's a satirical comment on our sick
society" I replied
"Whatever" she said "I don't hang out with racists" and moved
If that's the conclusion she drew from what I said

then

We're all doomed....

Pickin' my nose

Sometimes I pick my nose
Discreetly
Incognito
Hopin no one sees
        but not really caring if they do
I pull a veiny green one out
Inspect it
A sense of pride fills my heart
What a beautifully disgusting thing
        dangling off the edge of my finger
            like a leper from a ledge
I look around to make sure no ones watchin
          and wipe it on the wall
            beside me
             Not bad I think

Hangin my head out the streetcar

Hangin my head out the streetcar like a dog out the window
Wondering why a gurl is runnin full tilt to catch the cross walk
Where does she need to go so fast a 10 o'clock at night?
Joe Shuster's Way
10 people get out and start moving
Towards something
I don't know
Tow trucks pull cars away
  as some unlucky bastard whistles songs from his childhood
Cabs honk at each other like assholes pop farts
Countless people walk in a direction of content
The world laughs like the clouds smile with teeth of pure fluff
Biting chunks of nothing for no reason
I let the wind blow on my face
                and watch the tight jean hotties pull their pants up
Waiting for the last stop
Life's good
Real good

the wasteder I get

Two native girls walk on the streetcar
                                with a white guy
                                        covered in jailhouse
                                                tattoo's
They look like they've had a few
                        Faces worn by the years like good leather
They complain about their friend
                who sucked a "Black Guys Dick"
                while her actual boyfriend was in prison
The guy starts roaring out of nowhere like a handicap lion and
screams "Shut up, shut up your mouth"
He moves beside me
                and begins punching the seat like a mad man
One of the girls says "Friday the 13th that bitch is gonna get it"
The other one says "the wasteder I get the better I get"
I slowly get outta my seat and walk to the front on the
Streetcar like a coward
One thing I've learned in life
                        is never fight someone
                                with nothing to lose
                                        cuz you'll be the
                                                only one
                                                    losing

53

Go Train of Sleeping Death

On the "Go" train north headin to Barrie up top in the quiet
section
Everyone seated nicely with their heads back
Necks exposed
Ripe for a lunatic's blade
Nodding in an out of sleep
Holding on tightly to their phones
Only stirred when a text message comes in as they wake up for
a second to check it
Some listen to music
Others stare out the window not unlike a patient in an asylum
How many years have been spent on these trains?
In this strange purgatory
How many years wasted waitin?
For what?
The job
The kids
So they can go to their cars and drive another 20 minutes to
get home to their favorite TV shows and take out food at their
big houses in the burbs
Rows and rows of them fly by
All livin the dream
The same dream
The sane dream
Somehow my insane reality of writing and music doesn't seem
so crazy
Impractical
Yes
but its the practical dreams that kill
Maybe not physically but spiritually
mentally and psychically
People dead at 40 without even knowing it
When they do finally realize it they're already on their
deathbeds
They go out kickin and SCREAMIN for more life
A different life
In their final moments they'll think about all that time they
spent doin something they hated
to pay for shit they never wanted
to prove to people they didn't know
how happy they were
That very moment when death happens they'll reflect

and know they wasted an entire life
Now tell me this
are you one of these people?
If so,
what are you doing about it?

The Toronto Star

Front page news
"Rob Ford Smokes Crack Again"
Side note "Raptors win 105-103"
A story about a mayor smoking crack is big news
On the back page of the paper is an article called
"Big Brother Busy Watching Canadians"
It's about the government illegally spying on its "free" citizens
and they're paying for it with their tax dollars
Don't you think a story about the Government grossly abusing
its power is a lot more newsworthy then a crack smokin Mayor?
People call for Rob Fords head because he smokes crack and
does nothing about Stephen Harper illegally spying or collecting
information on them for reasons unknown
People are disgusted with Rob Ford when in reality they should
be disgusted with themselves for not being aware of what's
actually happening in Canada
For not knowing what is worthy of front page news
or the real purpose of the media
versus
the perceived purpose of the media
Until people demand truth over entertainment
They will continue to live
                    unenlightened zombie human slave minded lives

Tenants

I'm
surrounded
by
insane
droolin
rotten one tooth wonders
Picasso
stained
tan brown
suede jumpshoot wearin
grey haired
polite
degenerate tenants including myself
in my apartment building
on Triller ave
in Parkdale

A lie is a conspiracy against yourself

Conspiracy

A collusion in plan

A cabal
A Confederacy
A Coven
A League
A plot
A fix
Treason

Its mortal enemy

the Truth

The Religion of Money

Magical pieces of paper
and metal
used to control every Man
Woman
and Child
Most spend the majority of their lives panning for it
Their entire lifestyle revolves around it
The more you got the better off you are
People with lots of it are worshipped and envied like Gods
Most people's aspirations involve having lots of it
Ask a person what their biggest dream is
and they'll say
            it's to be rich
To have an unlimited supply of this magical substance
            so they can buy
                        anything
                            they want
So they can give their children everything they never had
The nice stuff
Love is overrated
People murder each other everyday over it much like many
other religions
Children are abandoned for it
Animals made extinct by it
They take over countries and destroy the World for it
Wars are funded on both sides by this
So are Governments
Corporations and Armies
Everything in the World runs on it
What do people praise more then Money?
Would you work for anything other then Money?
What has more admirers?
Jesus or Money?
Gandhi or Money?
The Prophet or Money?
Buddha or Money?
There is no bigger Religion then Money
Your entire life is dictated by Money
Most of the decisions you make takes money into consideration
Once you realize this
then maybe
you'll understand you're a slave to it

which means
you are a slave
and money
is your God
Now that you know this
Are you gonna continue to worship at its alter?

Frauds

For the most part people are frauds
Images of what they think they should be
Nothing very authentic
They use other people's words and slangs as there own
They copy their haircuts from people they look up to on TV
They measure beauty the same way
They have comic book and sports hero's they pretend they are
They imagine themselves on stage
                    like Cobain crushing his guitar
                            while screaming and shaking
                                    a generations soul
You picture yourself as Travis Prostrana
                                        doing the double backflip
                    The feelin he must of had
You're Eli Manning when he makes his great escape
                    and launches himself into the stratosphere
                                of the mind of western man
Rarely do you picture yourself as your Dad
                        punchin in and out everyday
                            to feed kids who don't appreciate
                                a thing he does
            No you forget many of the mundane little things
                        that in the long run of your life
                                are the most important things
                                that have and will ever
                                    happen
                                        to
                                        yourself

I Hate the Truth

The truth is
most people
when facing it
crumble into pathetic messes
The brevity
The reality of it
                is almost intolerable
It's like bein told you have HIV
Unbelievable at first
        but as time rolls on
            you either accept
                or ignore it
Naturally you hate the person who told you
Sometimes
        they have no other option
                            other than to lay it on you
                When they do
you must listen to it
Absorb it
Understand it
Figure out where it came from
                    and make amends for it
It's the greatest gift you'll ever get
                Sadly
                most
                people
            just wanna
                put
                their
            white ear
            buds in
                and
                skip
                to
                the
                next
                song

The Whiteman Inheritance

Where does white people's racism come from?
If a White person has sex with a person of colour
                  does the kid come out
                                      more white or coloured?
What about a White person and a Black person?
                        or an Indian person?
                        or an Asian?
                        or a Spaniard?
                        or any person of Colour?
   The majority of the time they look more coloured then white

   White people could fuck their race into oblivion
                                      and they know this

   White people have an inferiority complex
            You see we have a recessive gene
               The only way to deal with a recessive gene
                     is an oppressive regime
                              or
                     at least that's
                              what those in charge think
                     Sad view
                      true
                     but sad

Truth and Belief

There's no such thing
                as your truth
                            and my truth
                There is only truth
If everyone can have their own truth
                then truth
                        doesn't
                                exist
At one point the accepted truth was the world was flat
Now the truth is the world's round
The problem is people intertwine truth and belief
They think the words **Truth** and **Belief** are interchangeable
                        which
                            they
                            are
                            not
If you and I can decide what's right or wrong
then truth can't exist and neither can morality
Because our **"Truth's"** could be direct opposites
How can murder be right for you and wrong for me?
Circumstance or rationalization?
Truth is a compass not a GPS
You can't just plug in an address and go there
You need to use knowledge and deduction to determine it
The compass has 3 directions
Cause No Harm
Don't steal
Defend self from harm or theft
        Once you do this
                        you are truly living a moral life
No matter what you think
                    this is the truth
            and the truth cannot be denied
                IS
            the only thing
            that cannot
                be
            denied

Demoncracy, Lieberty and Freedumb

Is it worth the price?
Let's ask
Panama
Syria
Iraq
Afghanistan
Vietnam
Cambodia
Korea
Ukraine
Chile
Venezuela
Colombia
Cuba
Your mind
Soviet Union
The continent of Africa
if they like the gift
of democracy
liberty
and freedom?

Writing

Writing is dead
Books are dead
Thinking is dead
Writers are dead
Truth is dead
Opinion lives

Death

Marciano died in a plane crash
so did Richie Valens and Buddy Holly
Liston died of an overdose
even though he was
terrified of needles
and not a known drug taker
JFK was shot in the head
so was Lennon
Mao died of old age
Bukowski died of leukemia
Che was gunned down by a firing squad
Cobain used a shotgun just like Hemmingway
                              both shrouded in mystery
Escobar hunted down like an animal
Morrison died of an overdose
so did Ledger and Sid Vicious
and River Phoenix
and Layne Staley and, and, and
Johnny Cash died of a broken heart
The only difference between
the famous
and the unfamous
is
the famous
will have their
death's noted
on Wikipedia
The rest of us
will just
be names
on a Gravestone
if we're
lucky

Humans

Humans are the most adaptable creatures on earth
They can live in freezing temperatures
In the harshest climates
The worst terrain
They can live in deserts
On the moon
They can live in prisons with rape
They can live as the Humiliated and the Humiliator's
The Murdered and the Murderer
The Morale and the Depraved
The Conqueror and the Conquered
The Worshipped and Worshippers
They can lead while following
Live as Poetic Propagandists
Valiant Hypocrites
Inspiring Oppressors
as Sheep in Wolf clothing
That's what makes'em good slaves
That's what makes'em good masters

The Walls of Ukraine

Caught in a tug of war between East and West
Russia vs the E.U and the U.S
Communism vs Capitalism
Now America plays the Communist
or is it fascist?
Russia the Capitalist
or is it Socialist?
Doesn't matter
Either way
Both want to dominate
Want control
Want divide
Want conquer
Want peace
or is it submission?
Want what's neither of theirs
While the People burn
While the streets burn
While hearts burn
While water boils
While food runs out
While people fight
and die
While babies giggle
While Chernobyl is still unsafe
While Pelicans fish
and Crickets chirp
While the
devil
counts
sheep
the Politicians smile
with faces full of dollars
Pockets full of guts
Eyes full of kindness
and souls
full
of
Shit

A Beautiful State

Everything will run on time
No late subways or streetcars
All cars will be modified not to go more then 50 MPH
except the Police they can go a 100
No high speed crashes
No getaway drivers from jewel heists or bank robberies
No need to worry about food or housing
The Government will provide that for you
They've devised a dispensing system that allows them to ration
food based on supplies and needs
Three meals a day
No need to raise children
There's an institution dedicated to the education and
development of the child according to right conduct
You can visit during the holidays
Jobs will be a right not an entitlement
Everyone will work
Work as freedom
Entertainment beamed directly into your mind
War will be broadcasted as reality TV
Gladiator games returned to their former glory
Fights to the death
Sex will be celebrated as an expression of the oneness of all
beings with each other
No animal, child or tree will be left out
The food will taste fantastic and mixed with "essence"
the happiness drug
Visions of twisted light will be common place
Information will be free and everywhere
No need to use your brain because you can store your thoughts
on a disc or in cyberspace
A blank slate for the state to write on
The state
such
a beautiful state

Surveillance State

We don't live in a Surveillance state!
I mean what would that look like?
Camera's on every street corner
In elevators
Hall ways
Bank Machines
Stores
Police cars
Door ways
Most people have a video camera on their phone
Every person a potential rat
Organized crime must be terrified
                considering every person around has a device
                        in their pocket
                            that could be taping
                                    their every word
Imagine Donny Brasco but with a smart phone
You used to have to strap a mic to your chest
Now you just push a button on your phone
Everything you do is saved and uploaded onto a drive
Every text message
Every phone call in or out
Tracked
Your phone saves a record of your GPS routes
Your email and Facebook monitored
All your "Friends" or contacts known
If you don't think we're in a surveillance state
then tell me what is a Surveillance state?

The one thing all people have in common

The one thing all people have in common

Christian
Muslim
Hindu
Zoroastrian
Man
Woman
Child
Rock n Roller
Basketball player
Slave
Master
President
Prime Minister
Hitler
Mother Theresa
Ghandi
Jesus
Muhammad
your mom
Dad or brother
Sister
Aunt
Uncle
Bum
Rich
Poor
Powerful
Weak
Jeffrey Dalmer
Ted Bundy
Johnny Cash
Bukowski
Cobain
Writer
Good
Bad
Pretty
Ugly
is
we're all people

Old Whores Die Hard

Madonna
Elizabeth Taylor
Cher
Cleopatra
Mary Magdalene
Marie Antoinette
Rihanna
Tina Turner
Janis Joplin
Amy Winehouse
Hilary Clinton
Meryl Streep
Barbara Streisand
Your mother
Your wife
Your ego
Your sense of abandonment
Your cock
Your childhood dreams
Your youth
Your young ugliness and old beauty
Your nightmare job
Your meaningless conversations
Your MePhone
Your fuck you face
Your disposable dreams
Your stupid hairdo
Your dumb clothes
Your sense of entitlement
Your days wasted
        and your
           eyes purring

Christian Pagans

Constantine
The Merger
Christianity with Roman Paganism through the State
Christmas Trees
and Easter Bunnies
coinciding
with the Birth and resurrection of Christ
Winter solstice
Summer Solstice
Astrology
12 Months a year all named after Roman Gods or ideas
12 signs of the Zodiac
12 Apostles
12 Days of Christmas
12 Numbers on the clock
It seems there's a correlation between this
Is it possible most religions are based in Astrotheology
Monday (Lundi in French) is Moonday
Tuesday (Mardi in French) represents Mars
Wednesday (Mercredi in French) represents Mercury
Thursday (Jeudi) is Jupiterday
Friday (Vendredi) Venusday
Saturday (Samedi) Saturnday
Sunday represents the Sun
12 Major Greek Gods
12 Major Scales
12 Jury Members
12 Major Muscles
12 Major Organs
12 Minutes in a Basketball Quarter
12 Major Roman Gods
    All revolving around a central figure
    Jesus
    or the Sun
    or a judge
    or dial
    or Apollo
    or whatever

insignificant

My opinion is insignificant
So is yours
The Pope's as well
Same with Police Officers
and Lawyers
and Judges
and Doctors
and Actors
and Philosophers
and Writers
All insignificant
Opinion is
    a thought
        based
      in ignorance
     wrapped in personality
       molested by outsiders
     and spewed like shit
What matters is the truth
     and the truth
    cannot
      be
    denied
As the sun sets on your life
  it rises for someone else's
    and that's the truth!

A slave

A slave to cigarettes
A slave to booze
A slave to drugs
A slave to television
A slave to sex
A slave to the job
A slave to the girl
A slave to the family
A slave to fast food
A slave to soda
A slave to the corporations
A slave to the government
A slave to money
A slave to masturbation
A slave to the smart phone
A slave to propaganda
A slave to religion
A slave to god
A slave
A slave
A slave

Un Gringo en Medellin

The Streets of Panama

Running the streets of Panama with our driver Jorge
pronounced Whorhay
with my buddy Craig
thinking about my first book Dreg City
where I complain about the luxury of Canada
Now in Panama
Palm trees
Stray dogs
Old buses rammed to the teeth
Driven by what looks like a 17 year old boy
Some fat kid in tight white jeans hangs out the door
Jorge takes us to the Casino Fantastico
The houses appear to be one floor bungalow's cut out of
poverty
Rag tag roofs pieced together one sheet at a time
Most places are colored Van Gogh yellow
A man sleeps on a bench by his motorbike with a little bin
attached to the back
At the door stands a man in black fatigues
He scans us with a metal detector
Worry begins to seep in
My mind wanders
We're fucked if something goes wrong
Jorge is a Panamanian Gorilla
6 foot
300 pounds
Kind eyes
Warm smile
He could rip both of us to shreds and leave us for the dogs if he
wanted to
We sit down
Jorge orders us a bucket of "Panama" beers
Six for $10
Great price really
Football (soccer) on a huge projection screen
I ask him if he has any kids
He tells me he has 5 with one on the way
A family man
My nerves back off a bit
The Casino is filled with slot machines
People playing them
Surprisingly lots of Asian people in Panama

I think to myself who's playing who
Jorge tells us about Colombian Girls
He says they're bat shit crazy
He tells us about a time his Colombian girlfriend was sucking him off
She had suspected him of cheating
She took one of his balls in her mouth
Gripped it gently with her teeth and mumbled
"Who's Josephina" as she nipped at his ball
"Ahhh...what are you talking about?"
She bit down on his nut harder
"Who's Josephina?"
We all start laughin
He's just a guy like the rest of us
Looking to get a piece of ass and grind his way through life
We watch Football highlights
Drink our beers and head to the airport to catch our flight to Colombia
We pay him $30
Next stop Medellin

Mohalo

High up in the mountains of Medellin
looking at the city
8:30pm
It's as if God himself hangs here
The city lights look like stars beneath your feet
Dinking a Club Colombia cerveza
Smoking a cigarette
Xavier the owner of the bar welcomes and thanks us for
coming to his adopted city
He's originally from Barcelona
Long dusty grey hair
Warm smile
Happy soul
To look at a view like this every night would give anyone a
bit more soul
A half pipe sits on its own
I imagine skatin this thing
You might touch heaven with the right amount of air
Sitting at a table of twelve
All from different parts of the world
Kenton from America
California dirty blonde
Slow intelligent surfer drawl
A relaxing presence
Craig my friend from Canada
Shaved head
Handsome eyebrows
Seasoned traveler
Listens and tells stories of the road
Etha from Ireland
Gaelic speaking girl
Curly expressive hair like her personality
Big white smile

Cute sexy body
Nice 'lil ass
Brilliant open mind
Ellie one of 4 from New Zealand at the table
Tall brown hair
Long legs
Speaks very good Spanish
Young in body
Old in soul
Well informed
Strong woman who could hold her own with anyone
Cal sits beside me
Telling stories of free diving in Australia
He can hold his breath four minutes
His buddy five
It's a mental exercise more then anything else
Requires focus and calm
His teacher taught him to sing
"Smile and Breathe" after touching bottom
It relaxes you on the way back up
This leads to a conversation about the void
He and his friend are off to an animal sanctuary in Bolivia
The goal
To tie a jaguar or panther to themselves and take them for daily walks in an attempt to help reintroduce the animal to the wild
If the cat wants to climb a tree or go for a swim so do you
He tells a story about a guy he knows who did this
He ended up with a jaguar's mouth over his head
The cat was playing but his buddy was scared
He had to slowly slide his fingers into the cat's mouth and push his head out one terrifying inch at a time
It's inevitable to be scratched or bitten while doing this
Apparently there comes a point when something clicks and the cat accepts you

Stories of a documentary called "Christian the Lion" are told
I'm fascinated by the insanity of it all
These crazy people might be the sanest I've ever met
Strange how that works

Suzy

The most beautiful gurl
Curves like the mountains of Colombia
Lips thick
Painted red
Juicy
Voice of a Spanish angel
It moves
          when she says "Gringo"
Eyes brown like autumn leaves in Canada
Business owner
Her arepas are magnificent
chicken
chorizo sausage
beef
cheese
hand made guacamole
hot sauce
and the sexiest piece in Medellin serving them to you
Maybe God does exist
A club promoter
University student
Hard worker
Has lived in
Red Deer, Alberta
Toronto, Ontario
and Miami, Florida
Caramel skin
Soft silky flesh
I dream of Suzy
of Medellin
of Red
Yellow
and

Blue
I
dream
of
Colombia

The Cable Car

A bunch of us get on a sky lift goin to the top of Medellin
Mountains in every direction
Blue sky
Clouds
Wide Open Majesty
Then you look below see shacks
Shanty Huts made of scrap medal
Chickenwire fence windows
Poverty stacked on top of poverty surrounded by beauty
Out of nowhere
You see a massive cathedral right in the middle of slums
You also see jungle gyms
                          with kids playing and laughing on them
Kids on bikes ripping around the neighborhood
Playing Football
Having fun with each other
You see difficult conditions
                          balanced with happiness and good
A strange dichotomy
Sprawling beauty mixed with ugly poverty
Happiness in desperate circumstances
Even in rough conditions people are still happy
The other guys I was with saw a magical view and so did I
but it was the people who were greatest view of all

**A Whisper in the City
is Stronger
then a Voice
        in the Wilderness**

My Time

Of my time
Before my time
In my time

Ghetto Art

I met a mulatto guy in Chicago
outside a bar near Lincoln Park
He was short with relaxed hair
combed like Chuck Berry
He had this big toothy smile and a showman swagger
Heavy heeled platform shoes like Prince
A real old school feel to him
He'd approach people outside bars
and try to sell them art
He created these weird crayon filled pictures
on 8 by 11 paper
and'd sing with a 1950's Little Richard twang

"You wanna see some art?" he'd accent all statements with an

"Owwww….."

"Sure"

He'd pull out a picture of a dog eating bananas and say

"What, Dogs don't eat bananas"

Then in that high pitched rock n roll twang he'd scream

"Ghetto Art"

Then he'd pull out another drawing

"A Girl gets busted peeing in the alley"

"Ghetto Art"

"Whooaa….Kim Jong Un, I'm the bomb"

"Ghetto Art"

"Billy Dee Williams
Star wars what?"

And he'd sing

"I'm a Hustler baby"
just like the Jay Z song topped of with a "Ghetto Art"

"Lance Armstrong
interviewed by Oprah
Why did you cheat?"

"Ghetto Art"

"Tom Cruise in a Space ship
His girl is leavin him
The kid don't know what's goin on"

"Ghetto art"

I bought 2 pictures from him and moved on
Chicago thank you for this strange trip

The Imbecile is a Buddhist

A big man wearing a green fisherman hat
and red shirt with a yellow star
A dumb look and a communist to boot
He's lugging three large carry on bags
Stumbling around like a drunk mule
He has an equally unimpressive friend following close behind
He searches for his seat
Finds it and attempts to store his bags unsuccessfully
It's like watching a fat man perform ballet
No matter how good you might be you still suck
A complete fail
His friend tries to help him and succeeds at proving his own ineptness
The whole time they're bumping into people and making unnecessary noise
The people around him are staring at each other with annoyance and disgust
And hurry the fuck up faces
Kind of like watching a handicap person eat in a food court
If this was Rome they'd of had him crucified
A mob sufferers annoyance very lightly
Finally the stewardess comes to assist with storing his bags
Once she's done
He tells her someone is sitting in his seat
The stewardess asks the person to move
It's Unbearable
He sits down and starts talking about Ganesh and Vishnu
The Imbecile is a Buddhist as well
I think about immolation
I think about what it's like to suffer fools
                              who don't know they're fools
              He combs his hair
I feel sorry for him
He's just like anybody else
feeling his way through a dark room full of razor blades
Never thinking to use his eyes or mind to maneuver the dangers
He just walks and wobbles like the idiot he is

Mouse in my apartment

What should I do?
Get a trap?
Those cruel little chicken hawk devices
Maybe a glue trap with some peanut butter in the middle
I could see the little guy scurrying for some food
Sniffing with its cute lil nose
Catching the scent
A feeling of exuberance and anticipation taking over the whole
of its being
Thinking to itself
"Fucking pay day baby"
Feasts on the peanut butter
then
What's this?
It can't move
Panic
and terror set in
The more it struggles the more trapped it gets

Soon it loses all energy

Starving

Thursty

Angry and bitter

No longer able to move

Depressed and bored

the mouse

painfully

waits

for

death

So many people

So many people think once they get something
something else will happen
Once I get the condo
I'll get the gurls
or once I get the promotion
I'll get the respect
or once I get my haircut or new clothes
or shoes or a new song or poem
I'll get adulation
If you can't get gurls
respect
and adulation
before you get the new condo
or haircut or promotion
or shows or new songs
or poems or whatever
You won't get them after

The Oscars

Bet u a beer Leo or Mcconaughey win
not that Ejiofor
Altho it seems when someone plays a slave
they tend to win somethin
It's like the powers that be want to celebrate slavery
Leo's character in "Wolf" is a different kind of slave
A slave to money
and
all
the
good
durty
weird
beautiful
ugly shit
The hi's lo's
and eventual prison sentence
that comes with it
He is the American Dream gone bad
He is America embodied in one character
He is the death of the Dream
He is a prophetic vision of the fall of America
Profit over morality
Come to think of it
that's why he won't win
Cuz
the truth
no longer wins
in
Amurica

Most People

I don't like most people
I don't like their eyes
or their teeth
I don't like their clothes
or their conversations
I don't like their uninformed or misinformed opinions
I don't like their religions or ideas
I do like some things
I like their pussies and their tits
and their asses
and their little schoolgurl giggles
and their smells
their walks, ticks and wiggles
their eyes when they smile
The way they make your belly feel
I like their arms around me
I like their softness
I like their quirky personalities
I like them more if they like Bukowski
I like them more then they like me
Me
the mean funny man
with ego spun mood swings
ugly fool
lucky to be around
all these
beautiful
creatures
these
sexy
little
absurdities

Rebirth

Maybe rebirth is simply having kids
Living the lessons of the parents or the lack there of
All the lessons
and loathing and degeneracy's
and fucked-up-ness seething through the being of the child
Your future is your child
and the children are dying
enslaved
angry
people
wondering where it all went wrong
This life they have
Lessons unlearned
Sitting in the gutters of their parents slums
Puking up shit
Fucking whores
Drinkin swish
Waitin to die

Maybe

but

maybe

not

The _____ and the Doomed

Crazed
Beautiful
Young
Confused
old
All
Rich
Poor
Ugly
Horny
Free
Angry
The Doom
Normal
Equal
Elite
Everything
Leave it blank?

Dads

I talked my friend Jess at the bar the other day
She's a waitress
23 years old
I'm a regular and we hadn't seen each other in a while
She asked what I was up to
I told I was just finishing my first book "Dreg City"
and I had a show coming up June 7th
I was happy to see
                        she was genuinely interested
                                     in what I had to say
She told me she was in Victoria, BC for a wedding
She's originally from there
I asked if she missed home
She told me she didn't miss the city but she missed her family
In particular her Dad
I told her I only see my Dad twice a year
                         and everytime I leave him
                            it makes me sad
                    She agreed
                    and told me
                    how she
                  remembered
                    her dad
                being so strong
                  when she
                was young
                and now
                  he's
              73 years old
She was a love child from a 2nd marriage
Now he just gets greyer and greyer
I think about a picture of my Dad
                         holding up a salmon he caught in BC
           Big smile on his face
I get teary eyed so I stop thinking about it
She tells me how she also gets upset when she has to leave
She can't help bawling every time she has to go
I understand the feeling completely
but I'm a man
so I can't cry

I just feel a deep pain in my heart
I bottle it up
and I send it down to my pinky toe for later
I'll cry when I'm alone
It's safer that way
Our conversation makes me think about Dads
How they start off as all knowing God men
with super strength
and MacGyver like intelligence
only to end up human
Mortal but somehow immortal while they're alive
I think about Bukowski's Dad
and wonder why
he was such a terrible person
I feel bad for Bukowski
or anyone who hasn't had the blessing of a good Father
A Human Father
A Dad who's not afraid to put his arms around you

and say

"I Love you"

The Winters Itch

Like an itch this winter just won't go away
It seems the groundhog has killed himself
                              or at the very least is in a coma
The mood in the street is bitter
The office cold
The soul in need of chicken soup
Nipples always hard but the clothes are too thick to notice them
Snow in April
Wearing gloves and toques in May
Anger and despair epidemic
This is the kind of weather people die in
Loathing yourself in warm temperatures is one thing
            but couple loathing and freezing
                                    and you get suicide
People can't get passed the present
They think it'll be the same forever
Patience is a lying whore of a cheatin wife
They think the world won't change
Then it does
        and all those terrible thoughts go away
At least until it gets too hot
                    Then they'll complain about that

Old Tibetan Guy

I saw this short old Tibetan guy in the elevator
He wore a tan straight brimmed cowboy hat
      with a long thick grey braided ponytail
Cracked light brown weathered face
Holding onto what looks like a rosary but it's not
My lack of Tibetan theology is apparent
He's also wearing what looks like a multi-colored poncho
I stand behind him and watch the floors tick by
I notice a decent size bug crawling on his shoulder
 Like a grayish cockroach
My face squishes in silent revulsion
He gets off on the 12 floor
I get off a few floors later and walk towards my apartment
I see a door cracked open just slightly
A mulatto dude with thin corn rows
baggy jeans and a turquoise basketball jersey
peaks at me
He looks like he shouldn't be there
I watch over my shoulder as I pass by
Look him right in the eye and nod
He does nothing
I know he sees me
I don't like him
I go into my apartment and close the door
All this in the span of 5 minutes
No wonder I never wanna leave my place

Kerouac

or should I say Prince Myshkin
    stumbling
       through life
some how finding a key to high society
    thought himself
        the fool
chasing muses
  through colliding lives
in the great moment
    of time

Pigeons

Gross disgusting animals
Full of disease and death
Busts its ass 14 hours a day
7 days a week
scrounging for food
Fearless little fuckers
Tip towing around its human dependents
Cooing on store tops
Pooping on patrons
The punk rock embodiment of the animal kingdom
Doesn't give a fuck what anyone thinks
Will go on until the world
    has crushed the last piece of life
      out of it's vile beautiful self

Ubiquitous Cell

Cell phones
Smart phones
Old phones
New phones
Broken phones
Fancy phones
Loud phones
Annoying phones
Ugly phones
Out of style phones
Used phones
Sexy phones
Curvy phones
Fat phones
Phone phones
Phones are like people
                    but deader

**Listen to all
Follow one
Yourself**

I'm a Lion

I'm a Lion and this world is my Safari
I dominate with a calm easy demeanor
The young lions respect my grey bush
I laze around daydreaming about gurls and greatness
I rip meat from the bone
Mark my territory with a long gaze and serious look
I'm always seeking new lands
Sometimes people pull up in cars and stare at me
Uneased by my menacing freedom
They roll their windows up and pray I don't come any closer
They tell all their friends they saw a lion from 5 feet away
While they can't even see themselves
                                   from inside their own heads
        they dream of being a lion
                             while waiting for time to eat them

Views

I've seen some pretty spectacular views in my life
Mountains drippin with clouds filled in with water color blues
Like a pretty gurls eyes
Until you start walking in it
Mud gets all over your shoes and pants
Your feet get wet
It starts raining as you're tracking up the mountain
The terrain is rough
Each step becomes a mission in itself
Your picturesque view becomes your quintessential nightmare
The fucken irony
Beauty is best viewed from a far
The closer you get the uglier it becomes

10,000 Hours

The say once you've put 10,000 hours into something
you become a genius at it
The Beatles in Munich
playing 4 live shows a night
7 days a week
for 2 years
then invading America
Jimi Hendrix practiced 18 hours a day
for 10 years
Learned how to play on a 1 string Ukulele
which he could play any song on the radio
by tuning the string while plucking the note simultaneously
What do people put 10,000 hours into nowadays?
Warcraft
Television
Their Phones
Driving in traffic
Commuting
A nine to five
Watching porn
Watching sports
Listening to meaningless commentary
Commercials
Scratching their balls
Sniffing their own farts
High
Drunk
Being slaves to a system set up to make them fail
          but feel like they're winning all the fucken time
What have you spent 10,000 hours on?
What is your genius?
          If you could redo your 10,000 hours
                    would you dedicate yourself
                         to something that mattered to you?
               Hour one starts now

The Stones

Explored the blues
Played covers live
Saw the reaction
          adopted the style
Conquered it
Wrote blues inspired Rock n Roll
Sold millions of records
Became wealthy and influential
Wrote hit songs for years
Thought themselves Gods
Started indulging too much
Booze
Heroin
Sex
Cocaine
Egomania
Decadence
Aged
While death waits at the crossroads for his due

Civilization and Art

First art is pioneered
The Blues in Rock n Roll terms
It develops authentically
Then it invades like the Beatles and takes over
Then it becomes commerce and is sold
Then the formula changes
It takes on new forms
like
Rock n Roll
Punk Rock
It becomes abundant and influences the direction of society
Then it's intellectualized
                  formulas established
You understand what the people want
              how to present it to them
                  and feed it to them by the gallon
  It becomes decadent and fake
Sexualized
Debauched
      like Hair Metal or Rap nowadays
Then it consumes itself
        thinking it's saving itself
Then something else comes along and destroys it
         only for the cycle to repeat
               over and over
                  forever
  Like a never-ending line of dominoes
    one knocking over the other
    click
       click
    click
      .
       .
       .
        .
        .
       .

Artists of God

Fans are the worshippers
Rock stars are Gods
Lyrics are the words to live by
Music is the entertainment to keep the people in the pews
The message is repeated and repeated
The Managers are the Priests
The Keepers
The Setteruppers of the faith
Fans buy tickets
Parishioners make donations
Stars are idolized
Gods are worshipped
People aspire to be like them
Gods die
So do Rock Stars
Some Gods will be remembered forever
Rock Stars too
Fans sing along to the music
Worshippers sing hymns
Both get caught up in the myths
The Legends
The Stories
They lap it up like Vedder (My friends Rottweiler) does water
Both are excuses to lose your mind
Let go of everything
Find a warm place
Close your eyes
and fly
        fly away

Imagine

Imagine Prince Charles naked
Now imagine Napoleon
                    standing naked beside him
                        coverin up his little French weenie
Now imagine Hitler standing naked beside them
and Ghandi
and Malcolm X and Jesus all naked
Now imagine yourself naked
and your father naked
All standing in a line
No titles
No clothes to set you apart
No stature
Naked for everyone to see
What would people see?
Monsters?
Saviors?
Hero's?
Villains?
Great Leaders?
No
They'd see Men
Nothin else
We're all born equal
and
we all die equal
naked
and alone

God, if anything

Imagine you're immortal
Now imagine you're God
Now imagine you live in a box any size you want
Now imagine being in a tiny black coffin size box
Now imagine living in a huge football field box
Now imagine the box is as big as New York
Now Imagine the box is the size of the Milky Way
With anyone and anything you want in it
You create all the ideas
Everything in the box is an extension of you
You know everything going on with every plant
animal
star
galaxy
bug
fish
amoeba
man
women
alien
equation
blade of grass
You know all their thoughts
feelings
pasts and futures
every experience for the whole of time
Then imagine how boring that would be
Neitzche said God is dead
and I say
God,
if anything
is bored

Trouble

If the eyes of nature
          and the eyes of God
                    and the eyes of man
      don't see the same thing
    We're
     all
      in
       trouble

The King and The Man

A plane crashes on some remote island
Eight survivors live
One of the survivors takes over
Makes himself King
He claims the land as his own
Creates a flag
His minions build a castle
                        and farm for him
He reproduces with the women
They do this 40 years
In the 41st year they are re-discovered by the outside world
Long thought dead the self proclaimed "rescuers" cheer and say
"We've saved you"
They offer to take the King back to his old life
Just another animal on the farm
A working class biff
The King demands the outsiders to leave his land
               and to bring
                   an emissary
                       of their government
                 to see him
An Ambassador comes
The King tells the Ambassador
"This is My land
       My Kingdom
       My Country
       I own everything in it
       From the assholes on the animals
                      to the trees and minerals
     From the land to the sea
                   to the humans beneath me"
     The Ambassador responds
"Yes your Highness of course how can I be of service to you?"
"Leave" says the King
He does
The next day an army storms the beach
Conquers the land
Captures the King
Kills all the Kings men
              descendants
                 and family

The King realizes he's no King
Never has been a King
Never will be a King
Even if the whole world thinks he's a King
He's not a King
He's a man
A terrible
damned
disgusting
man
    who has
        earned
            his
        fate

The Hardest

Even the hardest criminal motherfuckers
                                    cradle their babies
                    Whether it's a serial killer
                        Gang banger
                        Military General
                President
                            Rapist
                    Diddler
                        Mass murderer
                Monster
                        Thief
                Torturer
                        Executioner
They will still quietly rock their babies in their arms

Future Teller

I can predict anyone's future
I don't care where ur from
What ur political beliefs are
What century ur from
What colour of skin
Gender
Religion or belief system you have in place
Want to know what it is?

Death

If I die or should I say when?

If I die tragically
or unexpectedly
in a plane crash
or a nuclear explosion
of a volcano eruption
or of old age
or whatever
Don't be sad
I've already had a magnificent life
Have a big party
Listen to music
Order Triple 8 pizza
Get extra Greek wings
Drink
Smoke
BBQ
Tell stories of the crazy and not so crazy things we've done
Laugh
Cry
Reflect
Move on
Let the memories
              be a gift
                     you can go back and open
                              whenever you want

Bully's

What's this with Bully's?
Everybody's on their case
Athletes against bullying
The whole point of sport is to bully your opponent into submission until victory is achieved
Government
and Police officers
and the Military
are all bully's
Wars are started and ended by bully's
Bully's are challenges you face at all levels of life
Throughout your entire life
Bosses
Band mates
Sound guys
Friends
Friends of friends
Cops
Teachers
Gurlfriends
Parents
Siblings
7-11 clerks
Bus drivers
and so on
In elementary I had a bully
Troy Rolland
Long greasy black ponytail
Thick rimmed glasses like Paul from the Wonder Years
Buck teeth
An ugly turd of a person
Stole my chips
Pushed me around

'til I went to high school and forgot all about him
Then one day when I was 16 my friend and I were driving down Broad St. North
and
who do I see walking?
The man himself
Troy F'n Rolland
and right beside him
my chance at justice
He turns on to Elmview Rd
I tell my friend to follow him
We pull over
I get outta the car
"Hey Troy remember me?"
He nods his head
"You and I are gonna fight"
He nods his head and rushes me
The Basturd's still trying to get the upper hand after all these years
I throw one punch
Hit'em in the nose
He drops like he got shot
I kick him in the gut a couple times you know like on TV
"Next time you see me, you better run" I say
"I'm the bully now bitch"
Jumped in my buddy's car and left
Sweet lady redemption
I remember another time in High School I was trying to bully a guy
His name was Delaney Rediger
He had long brown hair to the middle of his back
Nicely kept
Wore glasses like Ozzy Osbourne
Looked like a heavier version of him
Quiet guy

We were in the locker room
I started buggin him
Can't remember exactly what I said
I called him a pussy or somethin
He got up in my grill
in front of all the guys
and said "Say that to my face"
So I called him a pussy to his face and pushed him
To my astonishment the fucker didn't budge an inch
He was solid as a rock
That's when I realized this wasn't Delaney's first trip to the
super market
He's gone shopping before
He threw a punch
Hit me in the chin and I went to sleep
Nobody fucked with Delaney after that
He also taught me a great life lesson
All bullies get their due in the end
Including me

My Blanket

I had this blanket when I was a kid
It was checkered in blue and white squares
I used to wear it like a cape and pretend I was Superman
I would jump off the couch and pretend I was flying
All I ever wanted to wear was my blanket as a cape
No pants
No underwear
My little skin tag penis floppin in the wind
Full of potential
I wore that blanket completely out
For many years I had no blanket
No best friend to accompany me in my sleep
or on my trips to the void
Until I was 12 years old where I found my next best friend
A black blanket with little orange wool woven throughout
It was made by my Great Grandma Kari
On those cold Saskatchewan nights I'd pull it over my head and
cry to myself wondering why life had to be so tough
It dried all my tears and lulled me to sleep
Like a portable womb
Slowly it wilted away like the edges of a stone from water
Memories are all that's left of my blanket and Great Grandma
That blanket lasted until I left my Dad's place when I was 20
Eastdown and Toronto bound
Onto the next stage of my life
Onto my next blanket which came to me when living 411
Duplex at Yonge and Eglinton
A plush beauty with the image of a sunset on it
Gurls loved how it felt
I still have that blanket now
Once it's gone I'll be gone
Somewhere
Anywhere
Nowhere

As I lay on my couch

As I lay on my couch thinking about life
naked
and stoned
with no reason to live
which is the best reason to live
I look around
at the TV
at the guitar encased in empty beer boxes
Cobain staring down like the Sun on the Earth
Approving with his judging eyes
Lighters
Empty glasses of water
Guitar picks
Nail clippers
Jeans lying on the ground like dirty bums in the street
Rustling blinds aided by the wind of a great lake
Middle of July
33 degrees
Watching the World Cup
Germany wins in extra minutes
Sweating
Hungry
Distracted by thoughts of misguided self esteem
I venture into the wilderness of my mind and see the disease of
my generation
Our generation
Your generation
All generations
The Ego
The voice in your head telling you what to do
What to think
What to wear
How to feel
How to react
How to fit in while standing out
Yes I'm aware of this simple minded parasite
So easily controlled by the fantasy box
by materialism
by the dream of being rich and famous
of being a somebody in a world of nobodies where you don't
even know you
This horrendous nightmare of the beautiful has a hold on you

on us
on the Serf
the Peasant
the Ordinary Man
on the bank tellers and bus drivers and city workers and
whores and teenage boys
on those capable of breath
It's important to recognize yourself before you judge others of
misdeeds because you're guilty of them to
A species of hypocrites
of sentient liars with divine taste
Oh you brutal killers and lazy sloths
can't you see yourself in your Government
In your news
In your mirror
In your bedroom
In your soul
In your eyes
In your head
In your heart
?
What are you?
Who are you?
Where are you?
Why are you?
When are you?
Do you know?
Will you take the steps to find out?
Yes
No
Maybe
Death

Him

His emaciated greatness was apparent in his walk
The stories he tells
His eyes
Those kind sad eyes drunk with angry despair
Looking past his veneer of personality
A great man in strange circumstances
I just liked being around him
When I think back on those insightful days
I learned so much from him
He always said "Fail at being you"
From that day forward I dropped my superficiality
Stopped trying to be something I'm not
                              to please somebody I don't know
I began pursuing the things I love
Music
Writing
Women
Booze
Traveling
Napping on weekends
Partying during the week
Avoiding sunlight and humanity for days
sometimes weeks at a time
I think about this Man
and realize
It's
me

Violently Alone

I stand alone with brutal victory or violent death
them or me
Realizing this
I crush his skull with a brick
The other one pulls out a knife
and me
with my brick
starring into his eyes
possessed by sinister freedom
begin to laugh
a mad insane laugh
It's a hell of a thing to fight two men to the death
and still have a chance at life
I feel invincible
The man spooks and I move towards him
He lunges at me and I launch the brick at his face
I hear teeth hit the ground like dry macaroni
The greatest victories usually end when the violence does
As I look at the twisted flesh
I smile through the blood
Never feeling more alive
I walk home like a lion
majestic
free
and
violently alone

Acknowledgements:

This strange world

Contact Information

Matt Ross
therunge@live.com
Like me at www.facebook.com/inspiteofmygeneration

www.ingramcontent.com/pod-product-compliance
Lightning Source LLC
Chambersburg PA
CBHW070046100426
42740CB00013B/2817